Looking at . . .
Apatosaurus/Brontosaurus
A Dinosaur from the JURASSIC Period

Weekly Reader®
BOOKS

Published by arrangement with Gareth Stevens, Inc.
Newfield Publications is a federally registered trademark
of Newfield Publications, Inc. Weekly Reader is a federally
registered trademark of Weekly Reader Corporation.

Library of Congress Cataloging-in-Publication Data

Coleman, Graham, 1963-
    Looking at— Apatosaurus/Brontosaurus / written by Graham Coleman; illustrated by
Tony Gibbons. — North American ed.
        p.   cm. (The new dinosaur collection)
    Includes index.
    ISBN 0-8368-1273-5
    1. Apatosaurus—Juvenile literature. [1. Apatosaurus. 2. Dinosaurs.] I. Gibbons, Tony,
ill. II. Title. III. Title: Apatosaurus. IV. Series.
QE862.S3C62   1995
567.9'7—dc20   94-36809

This North American edition first published in 1995 by
Gareth Stevens Publishing
1555 North RiverCenter Drive, Suite 201
Milwaukee, Wisconsin 53212 USA

This U.S. edition © 1995 by Gareth Stevens, Inc. Created with original © 1994 by
Quartz Editorial Services, Premier House, 112 Station Road, Edgware HA8 7AQ U.K.

Consultant: Dr. David Norman, Director of the Sedgwick Museum of Geology,
University of Cambridge, England.

Additional artwork by Clare Herronneau.

Printed in the United States of America

Weekly Reader Books Presents

Looking at . . .
Apatosaurus/Brontosaurus
A Dinosaur from the JURASSIC Period

by Graham Coleman

Illustrated by Tony Gibbons

THE NEW
DINOSAUR
COLLECTION

Gareth Stevens Publishing
MILWAUKEE

Contents

Introducing
Apatosaurus

Once commonly called **Brontosaurus** (<u>BRON</u>-TOH-<u>SAW</u>-RUS), **Apatosaurus** (A-<u>PAT</u>-OH-<u>SAW</u>-RUS) had a body as massive as several elephants put together, along with a whiplash tail.

It would have towered above a human being — if any had existed at that time. But this was *not* the case, of course. And it would not have harmed you unless *you* provoked it.

So when did **Apatosaurus** live? What was the world like then? How intelligent was it? And who first discovered its remains?

Like other **Sauropods** — Apatosaurus was a huge, plant-eating dinosaur. **Apatosaurus** probably looks fierce to you because of its tremendous size, but it was more like a gentle giant and did not attack for food.

There are many facts to discover about this wonderful creature. We hope you will enjoy reading all about **Apatosaurus**.

5

Gentle giant

Weighing more than 20 tons — as much as four adult elephants —

To an **Apatosaurus**, you would have seemed as small as a house cat. In fact, **Sauropods** like **Apatosaurus** were the biggest creatures Earth has ever seen.

Apatosaurus was a huge animal. It had a bulky body and a long neck and tail. In fact, it was as long as two city buses — about 65 feet (20 meters). You would barely have reached above its shins, so you would have had to stretch your neck as far as possible to catch a glimpse of its head.

Wandering through the plains of what is now western North America, **Apatosaurus** lived in Late Jurassic times — about 145 million years ago.

Its head was very small compared to its body size, and its brain was tiny, too. That means it was probably not very intelligent, but it did not need to be. As a herbivore, it was happy spending its days browsing in the treetops for juicy leaves rather than stalking prey for its supper.

Its long, tapering tail was used for self-defense if an enemy approached. Wham! **Apatosaurus** would wield its tail like a whip to strike a nasty blow. It tried to knock fierce predators away.

Splendid

This excellent skeleton led U.S. president Woodrow Wilson to declare the 80 acres surrounding the area of its discovery, together with many other remains, as Dinosaur National Monument.

Remains found of **Apatosaurus** show it had a remarkable skeleton.

One of the best and most complete examples was discovered in Utah in 1909 by the scientist and dinosaur hunter Earl Douglass. It was later named **Apatosaurus louisae**, in honor of Louise, the wife of Andrew Carnegie. Carnegie was an American millionaire fascinated by dinosaurs. He donated money to build the Carnegie Museum of Natural History in Pittsburgh, Pennsylvania.

skeleton

The bones of **Apatosaurus**'s long neck were thick and strong. Its tail, meanwhile, which was even longer, narrowed from a wide base to a very slim tip. Try counting all those bones in its tail!

Apatosaurus's skull had eye sockets set far back, and there were long, slim teeth at the front of its snout — ideal for chopping leaves and plants.

The leg bones were extremely strong. They had to be to support all that body weight.

Scientists have found some **Apatosaurus** tracks that seem to be of their front limbs only. Scientists think these tracks are in places where lakes and rivers once existed and that these creatures may have been able to swim. They may have used their front legs to haul themselves along, while the rest of the body floated. Their tails helped propel them through the water.

One dinosaur,

During the so-called American "bone wars" of the late nineteenth century, scientists often fought over who would make a new discovery first, and many new kinds of dinosaurs were unearthed. One of the most famous paleontologists, Othniel C. Marsh, named one *Brontosaurus*, meaning "thunder reptile," because of the way he imagined its huge feet thundering on the ground.

Brontosaurus became one of the most famous of all the dinosaurs, catching the public's imagination because of its huge size. *Brontosaurus* also became the general term used for any huge **Sauropod**.

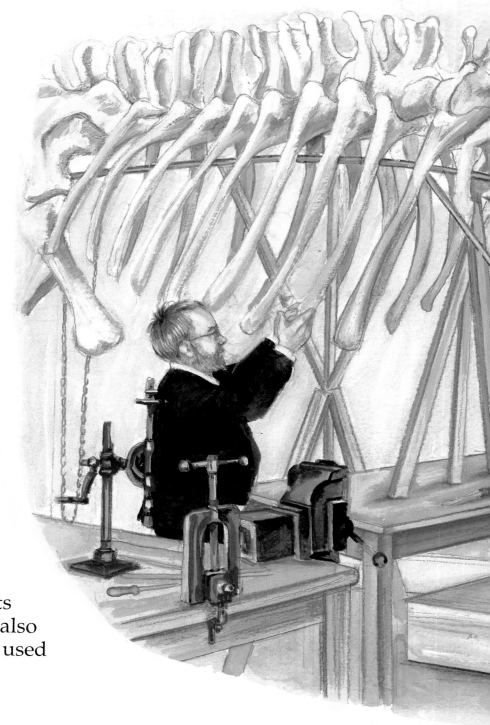

two names

The double use of this name was very confusing — even to the experts!

Today, however, we know that **Apatosaurus** and **Brontosaurus** were the same dinosaur, now officially called **Apatosaurus**.

The name *Apatosaurus* means "deceptive reptile." That's really a good name for a creature that once caused so much confusion to scientists and public alike, isn't it?

Here, you can see scientists putting together its skeletal remains, with the hips on the left.

Jurassic world

In Late Jurassic times, when **Apatosaurus** roamed vast plains between the forests and mountains of what is now North America, the weather was warmer and wetter than it is today.

Cycads, ferns, and ginkgoes, as well as horsetails and enormous conifers grew near swampy riverbanks. This lush vegetation was ideal for greedy plant-eaters.

As a herbivore, **Apatosaurus**'s main choice was between the low-lying plants that surrounded rivers and lakes and the leaves of tall trees. It had a very healthy appetite, eating tons of foliage each week. Luckily, it could skillfully cross stretches of water in search of more food on the other side.

Apatosaurus adventure

A herd of giant **Apatosaurus** was trudging through the Late Jurassic landscape, in search of new feeding grounds. As usual, the adults traveled on the outside

some of the adults seeing what was happening.

But the adults could not keep an eye on the curious youngsters all the time. On this warm, sunny

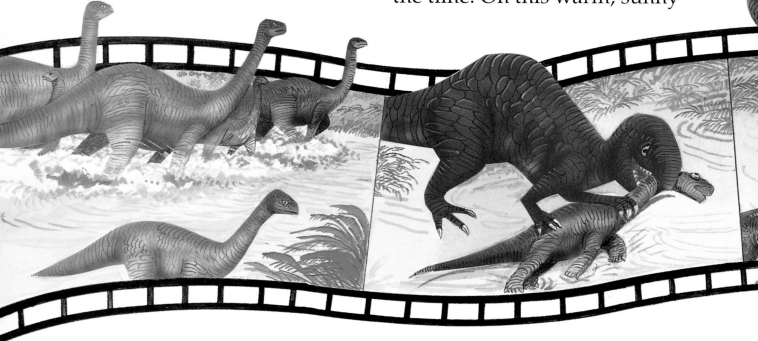

with the young in the middle. This way, speedy predators could not sneak up and attack the smaller **Apatosaurus** without at least

afternoon, one of them strayed from the herd to nibble some tasty looking ferns and drink from the river.

Just as it was about to snip off a snack, a fierce **Allosaurus** (<u>AL</u>-OH-<u>SAW</u>-RUS) leapt out. The young **Apatosaurus** froze in fright. Viciously, the **Allosaurus** knocked it onto its back and bit into its neck. The baby squealed in horror.

The hungry carnivore was about to kill its victim when a dark shadow fell across the ground. Suddenly, the **Allosaurus** was knocked away.

One of the largest adults in the herd had quietly approached while **Allosaurus** was not looking. It swung its mighty tail at the meat-eater, sending it crashing into nearby rocks.

The **Allosaurus** was stunned. So was the baby **Apatosaurus**. But after the adult licked its wound clean, the baby managed to walk again. Now, all it wanted was to return to the safety of the herd and rejoin the other young dinosaurs.

What was happening? The young **Apatosaurus** was being rescued by an alert adult.

It would not move away from the herd alone again until it was fully grown.

The prehistoric park that never was

So many dinosaurs and other prehistoric creatures had been dug up on the American continent that, back in 1868, some people decided to make a huge display of life-sized models in New York's Central Park.

Benjamin Waterhouse Hawkins, who had worked on the dinosaur models in London's Crystal Palace Park, was given the contract and began his research, producing a magnificent sketch of how everything would look.

The prehistoric park, however, was not to be. The city's government at the time was neither cooperative nor honest, and the project was suddenly abandoned.

The corrupt leader of the local council even sent vandals to destroy seven superb models Hawkins had already made. These wonderful reconstructions were broken to bits.

If *you* were given a chance to plan a prehistoric park now, which dinosaurs would you include? Which are your favorites? Today, some might even be robotic.

Dinosaur feet

Some dinosaur feet were wide and flat; some were narrow and had clawed toes. Others had hooves and soft protective pads.

Tyrannosaurus rex (TIE-RAN-OH-SAW-RUS RECKS) (2) had feet that were more than six times as long as yours! Each foot had three toes pointed forward, and one smaller toe pointed backward, not touching the ground. All its toes had sharp claws. The claws were often viciously used by this dinosaur for ripping apart an unfortunate victim.

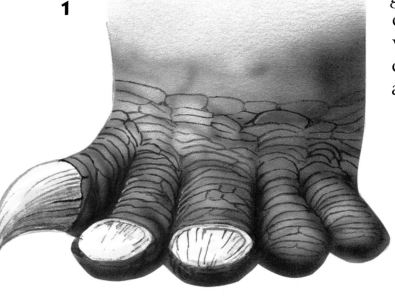

1

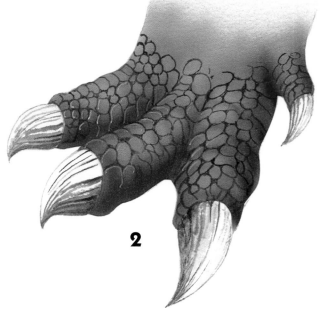

Apatosaurus (1) had wide feet with toes spread apart. This helped it support its great weight and keep its balance. One toe had a claw.

2

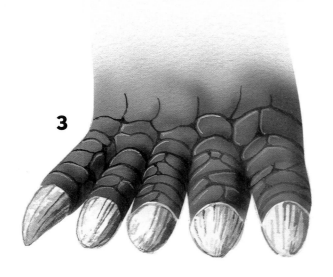

3

Stegosaurus (<u>STEG</u>-OH-<u>SAW</u>-RUS) (**3**) had five toes on each of its front feet and four on its back feet. Its short, hooflike claws could be used to help grip wet, muddy ground.

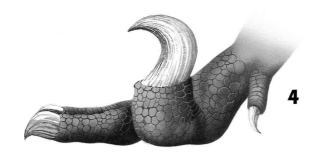

4

Deinonychus (<u>DIE</u>-NO-<u>NIKE</u>-US) (**4**) had four toes, although the first toe was small, backward-pointing, and not used much. The biggest claw was on the second toe. It was this vicious weapon that gave **Deinonychus** its name, meaning "terrible claw."

Gallimimus (<u>GAL</u>-EE-<u>MIME</u>-US) (**5**) had slim feet that helped it run very fast. Its toes were long and slender. The foot bones were even longer, like those of today's fast-running, ground-living birds, such as emus.

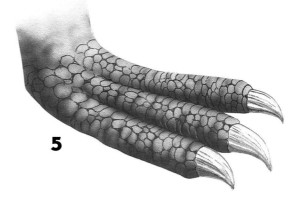

5

Triceratops (TRY-<u>SER</u>-A-TOPS) (**6**) had hooves on some of its toes. These protected its feet from rough ground. The back feet also had pads under them, just like those of rhinoceroses today, for comfort.

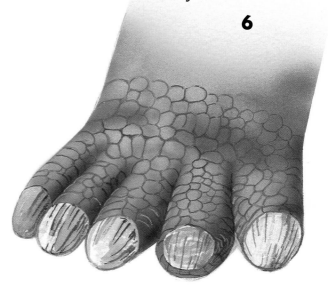

6

19

Apatosaurus data

Amazing neck

Apatosaurus could reach right up into the treetops to find the tallest branches. It must have had a powerful heart to pump blood through its colossal body and along that amazingly long neck to its head. And it must have had very strong muscles, too, to hold up that neck.

If you ever came across an **Apatosaurus** footprint, it would be wide and long enough for both you and a friend to sit down in together comfortably. Millions of years ago, **Apatosaurus** made footprints in the mud that were very deep and large because of its tremendous body weight. Here are some other fascinating facts about this typical **Sauropod**.

Small brain

Apatosaurus had a tiny brain for its body size. In fact, it was probably one hundred thousand times lighter than its total body weight. The chances are that it was not the most intelligent of creatures, in spite of its huge size.

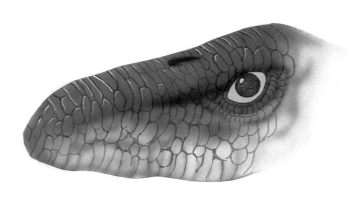

its food like humans do. Instead, it may have gulped down whole plants or clumps of leaves greedily. To aid digestion, it may also have swallowed small stones. These would have helped grind the food in its stomach.

Strangely placed nostrils

Most creatures have noses below their eyes — like you do. But look where **Apatosaurus** had its nostrils! Some scientists think that having nostrils so high may have helped **Apatosaurus** breathe when it entered the water.

Padded feet

Apatosaurus had four large, flat feet. Scientists think that, just as your own sneakers have padded soles,

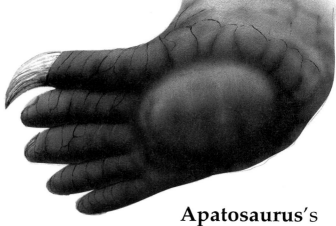

Weak teeth

Like most **Sauropods**, **Apatosaurus** had teeth only at the front of its mouth. They were long but not very strong. Scientists think **Apatosaurus** may not have chewed

Apatosaurus's feet had special padding inside. This padding acted as a cushion, providing support and preventing damage from the creature's extreme weight. Take a look, too, at the large claw on its inner toe. It was probably used as a defensive weapon.

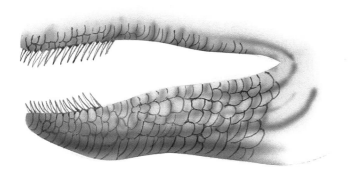

More of the Sauropod gang

Apatosaurus (1) was a typical **Sauropod** — a huge, four-footed plant-eater with a small head, a long neck, and a long tail.

Diplodocus (DIP-<u>LOD</u>-OH-KUS) (2) was another **Sauropod**. Its name means "double beam" because of a special feature of its backbone. **Diplodocus** lived in North America during the Jurassic Period. Although not as heavy as **Apatosaurus**, it was longer.

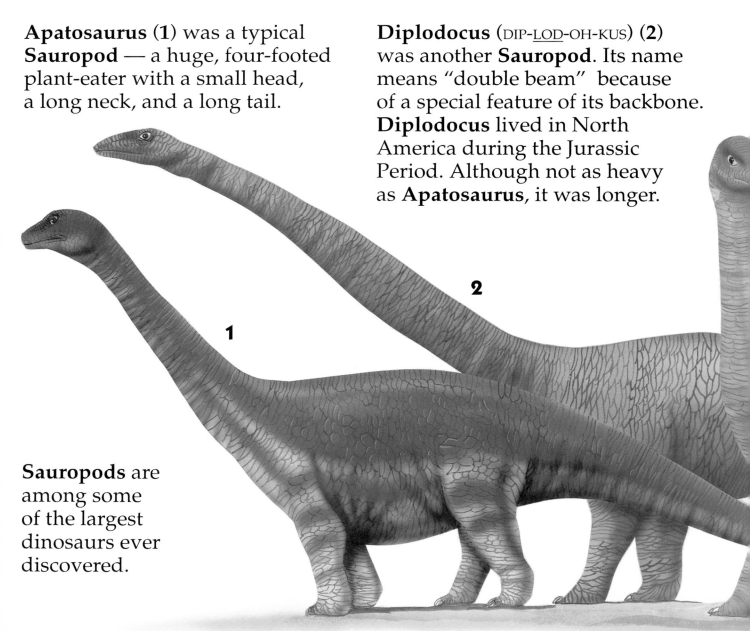

Sauropods are among some of the largest dinosaurs ever discovered.

Antarctosaurus (ANT-ARK-TOE-SAW-RUS) (**3**) lived in later Cretaceous times — about 70 million years ago — in what is now South America. It may have been twice as heavy as **Apatosaurus**, although not as long from the end of its snout to the tip of its tail. Its body must have been extremely heavy and bulky.

Dicraeosaurus (DICK-RAY-OH-SAW-RUS) (**4**) lived in Jurassic times in what is now Tanzania, in southeastern Africa. It was smaller in height and length than most of the **Sauropods**, and it weighed less than half a **Diplodocus**.

Some scientists have also guessed that these giant creatures may have had a life span of two hundred years. That's a very long time — almost three times as long as the average human lives today!

We can tell from tracks imprinted in mud and fossilized into rock that **Sauropods** usually traveled in herds. They probably migrated regularly, too, in search of new feeding grounds. They would move from place to place with the youngsters in the center of the herd as protection against predators.

3

4

GLOSSARY

carnivores — meat-eating animals.

conifers — woody shrubs or trees that bear their seeds in cones.

cycads — tropical shrubs or trees that look like thick-stemmed palms.

ginkgoes — trees with showy, fan-shaped leaves and yellow fruit.

herbivores — plant-eating animals.

paleontologists — scientists who study ancient remains of plants and animals.

predators — animals that capture and kill other animals for food.

prey — animals captured and killed for food by other animals.

propel — to make something move forward.

remains — a skeleton, bones, or a dead body.

INDEX